IPAD AIR 4 U

A Simplified Manual With Complete Step By Step Instructions For Beginners & Seniors On How To Operate The New iPad Air 4th Generation With iPadOS Tips And Tricks

BY

TERRY HARLEY

DISCLAIMER:

The information contained in this book is for educational purposes only. All efforts have been executed to present accurate, reliable, and up to date information. No warranties of any kind are implied. The contents of this book are derived from various sources. Please consult a licensed professional before attempting any techniques contained herein.

By reading this document, the reader agrees that under no circumstances is the author responsible for any losses, direct or indirect, which are incurred as a result of the information contained in this book including errors, omissions, and inaccuracy.

Table of Contents

INTRODUCTION

The Apple iPad Air 4th Generation is the next evolution of the Air tablet line. It has a 10.9-inch display, a Touch ID on the power button, and a powerful A14 Bionic processor. It is also compatible with the 2nd gen Magic Keyboard, Apple Pencil, and USB-C. It brings its power and form to the masses. The iPad Air is like a bridge between the 10.2-inch iPad and the 11-inch iPad Pro. The new design and improved chip blurs the line between standard and pro iPad.

FEATURES OF THE IPAD AIR 4

Design

The previous iPad Air models range in size from 10.5 inches to 10.9 inches. The 2020 iPad Air now includes an edge-to-edge display, identical to the one found on the iPad Pro. The aluminum frame wraps around the Retina display and features flat, rounded corners. This is the first design used for the Apple iPad pro.

The smaller body and thicker bezels surrounding the screen differentiate the iPad Air from the 11-inch iPad Pro.

iPad Pro left, iPad Air middle, iPad right

The former iPad Air was smoother and had a curved sharp edge; the new layout is thinner and more industrial, and it is compatible with the iPad Pro and iPhone 12 models.

It is the first iPad Air with all the display designs and no Touch ID Home Button. There is no Face ID, but, a new Touch ID with biometric authentication has been added to the top button via a fingerprint reader. It detects your fingerprint in the same way as the Touch ID Home button does, but it is much smaller and denser. The speakers and microphone are positioned on the top of the iPad Air near the Touch ID button.

The volume up and volume down buttons, a nano-SIM slot on the Cellular models, and magnetic spaces for charging the Apple Pencil are all located on the right side of the iPad Air. There is a single-lens rear camera with a microphone on the back, but there is no secondary camera or LiDAR scanner, unlike with the quad-shaped camera on the iPad Pro.

The dual speakers and USB-C port are located on the iPad Air's base.

Colors

The iPad Air's metallic exterior can be found in five colors, which marks the first time Apple has offered a non-traditional color to an iPad. The iPad Air has four colors which are space gray, rose gold, green, and light blue.

The dissimilarity between the 2020 iPad Air and the 2020 iPad Pro is the three vivid color options: rose gold, green, and light blue.

Touch ID

Touch ID, which was not integrated into the Home Button of the device home button, was originally launched on the iPad Air. The iPad Air now features Touch ID on the top button, allowing Touch ID-based biometric verification without the heavy bezels that impede the display.

The Touch ID top button unlocks your iPad in the same way that the Touch ID Home button does; it gives you access to apps and items purchased with Apple Pay. The touch ID on the iPad Air works in harmony with portrait and landscape orientation.

Smart Connector

The iPad Air's clever connection on the rear enables it to connect and charge gadgets like the Magic Keyboard. The Smart Connector interface transfers power and data;

Therefore, accessories connected to the iPad Air through the Smart Connector do not require batteries.

USB-C

Following the iPad Pro, the iPad Air is the second iPad to ditch the Lightning connector in favor of USB-C. The iPad Air has the capability to connect to 4K or 5K displays, cameras, and other USB-C devices because of its USB-C port. With the USB-C port, you can charge an iPhone and Apple Watch with the right cable and it also lets 5Gbps data transmission.

Display

The iPad Air has a 10.9-inch Liquid Retina display, same with iPad Pro, but lacking 120Hz ProMotion technology for a flatter scrolling experience.

The resolution varies from 2360 to 1640 at 246 pixels per inch, for a total of 3.8 million pixels. It features complete lamination (which reduces the size of the screen and makes the content look more realistic); Rich P3 Extensive color support with true-to-life colors; 500 nits, 1.8 percent anti-reflective coating, and True Tone support.

True Tone adjusts the screen's white balance to suit the ambient light, making the scene more relaxing to the eyes. The color of the display is warm in a room with yellow light, so the difference between the iPad and the room lighting is not obvious.

Apple Pencil Compatibility

The latest iPad Air is compatible with Apple's second-generation Apple Pencil, which was launched with the iPad Pro in 2018. Before the release of the iPad Air, the second generation Apple Pencil was only available for iPad Pro devices.

A14 Chip

In the iPad Air, Apple makes use of the newest 5-nanometer chip technology and a 6-core A14 Bionic processor. Apple generally doesn't implement the new chip technology in the iPad prior to putting it in the iPhone, but due to the late launch of the iPhone 12 series, this happened in 2020. The A14 Bionic chip in the iPhone 12 is the same as in the iPad Air 4.

 A14 Bionic

According to Apple, the A14 chip has 11.8 billion transistors, boosting performance and power efficiency. The design of the 6-core A14 chip increases the performance of the GPU by 40% compared to the A12, while the new 4-core GPU architecture improves the graphics performance by 30% compared to the A12.

The leaked A14 chip benchmark agrees that the fourth-generation iPad Air is a huge improvement when compared to the foregoing model. It has 1583 single-core and 4,188 multi-cores, which is faster than the 1112 single-core cores and 2,832 multi-cores obtained through the A12 Bionic chip on the 3-generation iPad Air.

1583

Single-Core Score

4198

Multi-Core Score

Geekbench 5.2.3 for iOS AArch64

Neural Engine

The A14 Bionic contains a 16-core Neural Engine that is twice as fast as the previous model; it can perform 11 trillion operations per second, allowing for faster machine learning capabilities than ever before. Machine learning has a second-generation accelerator in the CPU for 10 time's quicker machine learning Calculations.

Apple claims the new iPad is capably equipped with the improved GPU and A14 Neural Engine, such as photo identification, natural learning languages, movement analysis, and much more.

RAM

Based on the A14 mentioned above, the iPad Air has 4 GB of RAM, which is 3 GB more than the previous model, which is 1 GB.

Camera

Although the iPad Air lacks a TrueDepth camera system that enables Face ID, it does include a front-facing f/2.0 7-megapixel FaceTime HD camera for selfies and video chats.

On the back of the iPad Air is a 12-megapixel single-lens wide-angle camera, which is identical to the wide-angle camera on the iPad Pro. In comparison to the previous iPad Air, it enables high-resolution video and 4K video recording.

The 12-megapixel camera has an f/1.8 aperture for compact performance and is configured for low-light operation. It also has all the innovative camera features from Apple such as Live Photo with Stabilization, Auto Focus in Focus, Wide Color Capture, Exposure Control, Smart HDR, Auto Image Stabilization, Noise Reduction, and much more.

You can capture Slo-mo videos at 120 or 240 frames per second, while 4K videos can be captured at 20, 30, or 60 frames per second. The iPad Air captures at 1080p at 30 frames per second. It can also record at a 60-frame-per-second frame rate. It has continuous focus, cinematic video stability, and the ability to record 8-megapixel images while filming 4K video.

Battery Life

The iPad Air is powered by a lithium-polymer battery with a 28.6watt-hour capacity that can last up to 10 hours while browsing the web or watching videos via Wi-Fi.

Cellular models work for up to nine hours when accessing the Internet via a cellular connection. A 20-watt USB-C power adapter and a USB-C to USB-C connection are required to charge the iPad Air.

Other Features

Microphone and speaker

The iPad Air provides dual stereo audio in portrait and landscape mode. Two microphones are built-in for calls, recording video, and audio.

Sensors

iPad Air with Touch ID sensor Includes ambient light sensor for True Tone, accelerometer, barometer, and other functions.

Wi-Fi 6 and Bluetooth support

2020 iPad Air supports Wi-Fi 6, also known as 802.11ax. When numerous Wi-Fi devices are present in the same area, the enhanced standard provides quicker speed, increased network capacity, improved power efficiency, lower latency, and enhanced connection.

Wi-Fi 6 devices support WPA3. It has extended cryptographic strength for security. Bluetooth 5.0 compatibility is also available.

Gigabit LTE

On iPad Air cellular versions, Gigabit-class LTE is enabled. The LTE modem chip is the same as that used in the iPad Pro.

1, 2, 3, 4, 5, 7, 8, 11, 12, 13, 14, 17, 18, 19, 20, 21, 25, 26, 29, 30, 34, 38, 39, 40, 41, 46, 48, 66, 71 are Routes that are all supported.

The iPad Air has two options of SIM cards: Next to the device is a nano-SIM card slot and an eSIM or digital SIM to work without a physical SIM card.

The Nano-SIM physical card slot supports the Apple SIM card. It allows users to easily switch between carriers without a hassle. Most operators in the US and other countries support Apple SIMs. However, those that don't like Verizon require a physical SIM card.

Storage space

Apple sells the iPad Air with 64 GB or 256 GB of RAM, however, 128 GB is not an option.

Accessories

Support for Magic Keyboard and Trackpad

The iPad Air, like the iPad Pro, is meant to operate with the Magic Keyboard, which was available in early 2020. For the first time, the Magic Keyboard incorporates a folio-style casing with a complete backlit keyboard and a trackpad.

The magic keyboard uses scissors mechanisms such as the MacBook Air and MacBook Pro. Apple says that the scissor mechanism travels 1 mm, providing the greatest typing experience ever on an iPad.

The iPad Air is attached to the magic keyboard through a magnetic link with a cantilevered hook working on your desk or lap. The hinges can adjust the viewing angle up to 130 degrees; therefore, they can be adjusted to any operating situation. The Magic Keyboard structure allows the iPad to "hang" in the air while in keyboard mode, with the lower part tilted backward.

When not used, the iPad Air is protected by the keyboard folio's front and back covers. The magic keyboard has a USB connector for USB-C passthrough inductive charging, freeing up the iPad Air's built-in USB-C connection for other devices such as external drives and displays.

Apple pencil

The second version of Apple Pencil is compatible with the 2020 iPad Air devices. The $ 129 Apple pencil links the iPad Air to the magnets and charges inductively when magnetically attached. Paring is also carried out through a magnetic attachment.

 Pencil

The second-generation Apple Pencil has gesture capability. You can suddenly change from a brush to an eraser with just a tap instead of picking up the pencil and choosing a new tool.

Apple Pencil works with first and third-party applications on the iPad Air. It offers improved palm rejection, incredible accuracy, and undetectable delay for a paper-like writing experience that no other styluses can match.

By increasing the pressure on the iPad screen, the pressure becomes thinner, and thicker lines can be drawn, and the side nib detection gives shade when tilting the Apple pencil.

CHAPTER 1

HOW TO SET UP YOUR NEW IPAD CORRECTLY

Congratulations - you brought a new iPad! You'll want to set up your new tablet as quickly as possible, whether it's the high-tech marvel of the new iPad Pro, the super-fast iPad Air, or the tiny iPad mini.

This manual will provide you with a variety of helpful hints and modifications to get you up and running with the new iPad as quickly as possible. From backing up your old iPad (if you already have one) to start over with the newest iPad, this guide is here to guard you.

Initial Setup

Auto setup for iPad

If both of your devices are running the most recent version of iOS, the automatic installation will function. By putting two devices close together, the automatic setup allows you to copy your Apple ID and home Wi-Fi settings from one to the other.

You can put them next to each other, follow the instructions, and skip inputting your Apple ID and Wi-Fi pin if your old iPad (or iPhone) is already running iOS 11 or later. This helps to make the first setup go more smoothly.

All of your applications and other data are transferred via automatic installation, making the setup procedure as simple as possible. You won't have to manually download any apps; they'll be available as soon as your new iPad is turned on. Want to start from scratch instead? Keep reading!

Begin setup.

This is great news because a Mac is not needed to set up a new iPad. Take it out of the box, remove all the plastic protective covering from the iPad and open it.

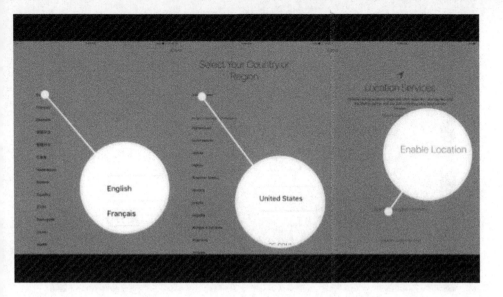

To frame everything, go through the setup screens one by one. Select your preferred language, followed by your preferred country or area. You'll be prompted to choose your Wi-Fi network and enter its password. Set up Face ID or Touch ID after activating location services with a tap.

The next step is to create a password, which is now set to a six-digit number by default. Click the password choices at the bottom of the screen if you wish to use less than four digits or a password/expression. If not, type in your six digits and then repeat to verify.

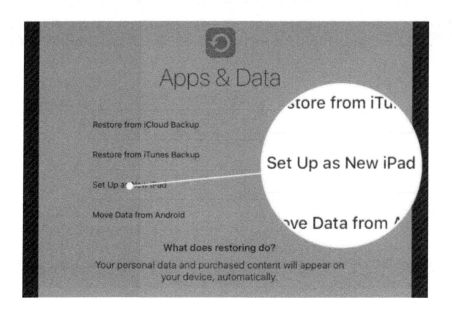

Choose one of these Restore choices on the Apps & Data page if you're backing up your old iPad to iCloud or iTunes. If you're beginning from scratch, select Set Up as a new iPad or Move Data from Android if you're approaching from the dark side.

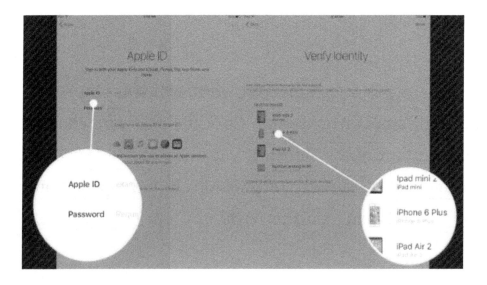

When you select Setup as New iPad, you will be taken to the Apple ID page. This is where you'll type your Apple ID and password. You must authenticate your identity with a trusted device if you've enabled Two-Factor Authentication on your Apple ID. You will receive a verification code on one of your other devices, which you must input on the iPad screen. To proceed, accept the terms and conditions after logging in.

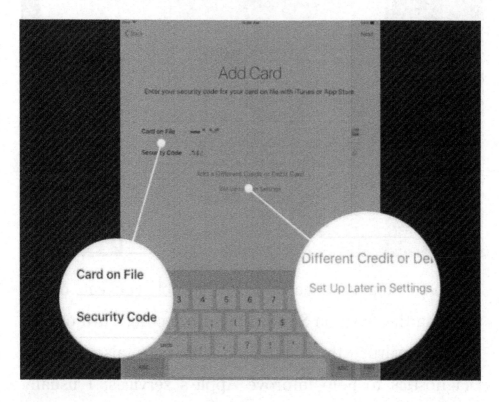

After that, you'll have the option to set up Apple Pay. If you have an Apple Pay card in your iCloud account, click the Next button at the top corner of your iPad screen to bring up the Add Card page, which will be filled with your default Apple Pay credit card. Enter the Security Code that has been requested. If you don't have Apple Pay set up yet, input the card information in the spaces given, or go to Settings and choose Setup Later.

The next step is to activate Siri, which you can do by pressing the Turn on Siri screen or selecting Turn on Siri Later towards the bottom. You can also submit Diagnostics to help improve Apple's services; I usually send them to Apple, but some privacy enthusiasts don't. It's all up to you. The same is true when it comes to sharing app analytics with developers.

Configure Your iPad

You'll see all of your iPad's applications, including Messages, Mail, Reminders, and News, when you arrive at the home screen. Tap and hold any icon and it will all start wiggling. To place the icons on the second (or third or fourth) page, you can tap and drag the screen to arrange them in a way that makes you very happy.

Next, go to the App Store to get any applications you currently own for free on your new iPad by tapping the Purchased button below. Most iPhone applications have a matching iPad app, which can be found under the Purchased tab. Tap it with the down arrow on the little cloud to get your new device.

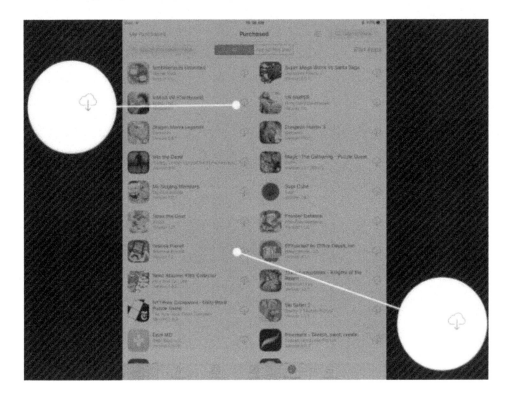

CHAPTER 2

FUNDAMENTALS

Setup Touch ID on your iPad

Utilize Touch ID to open your device conveniently, verify purchases and payments & login to third-party applications when you press the top button.

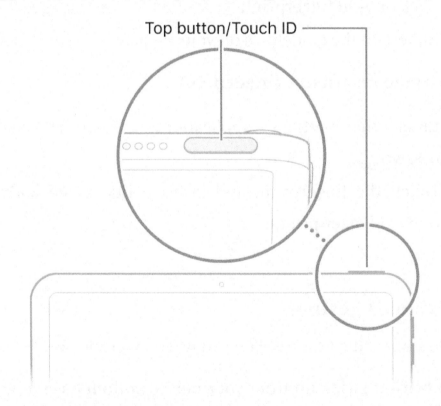

Top button/Touch ID

- If you did not activate access to your fingerprint when you first setup your iPad, enter the Setting application> Touch ID and Passcode.

- Activate any option, and adhere to the directives on your display.

To add a fingerprint

You can add more than one fingerprint.

- Enter the Settings application> Touch ID and password.
- Click on Add fingerprint.
- Adhere to the guidelines on your display.

To name or erase a fingerprint

- Enter the Settings application> Touch ID and password.
- Touch the fingerprint, and insert a title or click the remove Finger print icon.

Advanced gestures

Below are some gestures you can use on your device.

Go home: swipe up from your device bottom edge to go back to the home screen whenever you want

Launch Control centre. Swipe down from the top right corner of your display to reveal the control centre; long-press a control to open more options of the control. Enter Settings> Control Center to add or erase controls.

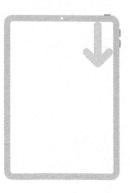

Launch the Application Switcher: Swipe up from the bottom edge of your display and stop at the middle of your display, and then raise your finger. Swipe to view all open applications.

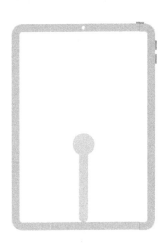

Launch the Dock in an application. Swipe up from the bottom part of your display & stop to open the Dock. Tap on any application in the Dock to launch the application.

Tell Siri. You can say, **Hey Siri**. Or hold down the top button and state what you want. Siri would listen to what you say till you free the button.

Snap your screen. Press and release the top & volume buttons at once.

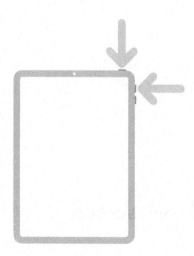

Set the date and time on your iPad

As a rule, the date and time displayed on the Lock screen are immediately determined depending on your location. You can fix it if it isn't correct

- Enter the Setting application> General> Date and Time.
- Activate any of the below:
  - ➢ Set Automatically
  - ➢ 24-hour time

Set region & language

- Enter the Settings application> General> Languages and regions.
- Set any of the below:
  - ➢ Language for iPad
  - ➢ Region
  - ➢ Format of calendar
  - ➢ Temperature unit

Access features from the iPad lock screen

- Launch camera: Swipe to the left.
- Launch the control centre: Swipe up from the upper right part of your display.
- View earlier alerts: swipe up from the middle
- Check out Today's view: swipe right.

- Begin to draw and take notes: use the Apple pencil to tap on the lock screen. Anything you make would be stored on the lock screen.

Change Wallpaper

- Enter the Settings application> Wallpaper> select a wallpaper.
- Do any of the below:
  - ➢ Select an image from the set of pictures at the top of your display.
  - ➢ Choose any of your pictures (click on an album, then click on the picture).
  - ➢ Click on Set, then select any of the below:
- Click on Set, and select any of the below:
  - ➢ Home screen
  - ➢ Lock screen
  - ➢ Both

Search with iPad

Search can be of aid in locating applications & contacts, searching inside applications such as messages & mails, etc.

Select which applications to add to Search

- Enter the Settings application> Siri and Search.
- Scroll down, click on an app, then activate or deactivate Show in Search.

To Search with iPad

- Swipe down from the center of your device's home screen.
- Click on the search box, then write whatever you want.
- Click on any of the results

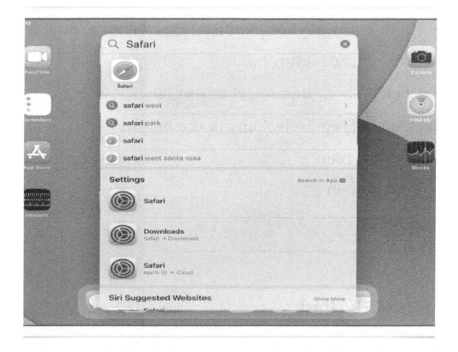

Dictate Text

Rather than typing on your device, you can simply dictate the text.

Ensure you activate Enable Dictation in the settings application> General> Keyboard.

To dictate

After activating Enable Dictation, click on the Dictate icon 🎤 on the on-screen keyboard, then state what you want.

When you are done, press the Keypad icon ⌨.

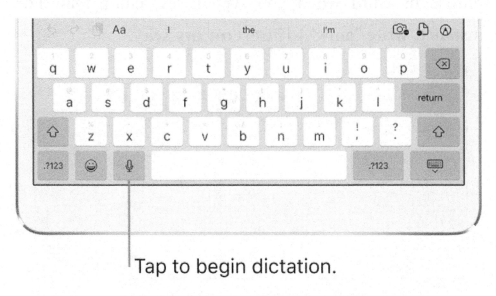

Tap to begin dictation.

To insert a text using dictate, click on where you want to put the insertion point, and then click the Dictate button 🎤.

To Add punctuation or text format

Say the formatting or punctuation while you dictate the text.

For instance, "Hello Bruce comma the letter is in the mail full stop" would become Hello Bruce, the letter is in the mail.

Text replacement

Create text replacement that can be used to insert a phrase or word when you type a few characters. For instance, write "omw" to insert **on my way**.

To make text substitutions

- Do any of the below:

- ➢ Using the on-screen keyboard: hold down the Emoji ☺, or Switch keypad button⊕, click on Keyboard setting, and then click on Text Replacement.
- ➢ Using an external keyboard: enter the Settings application> General> Keyboard, then click on Text Replacement.
- Touch + on the upper right.
- Insert a phrase in the phrase box and the shortcut you want to utilize in the shortcut box.

Adding or removing a keyboard

- Enter the Setting application> General> Keyboard.
- Click on keyboard, then do any of the below:
  - ➢ Adding a keyboard: click on Add new keyboard, and then select a keyboard from the catalog. Repeat the process to add more keyboards.
  - ➢ Erase a keyboard: Click on the edit button, click ⊖ beside the keyboard you plan on removing, click the Delete button, and then tap on Done.
  - ➢ Sort your keyboard catalog: click on the Edit button, slide the Edit button ≡ beside any keyboard to a new location in the list, and click on the Done button.

To Switch to another keyboard

- On the keyboard: hold down the Emoji key☺, or the Switch keypad key⊕, and then click on the keyboard you want to change to.

AirDrop

With AirDrop, you can transfer your photos, videos, sites, location, etc. to devices and Macs close to you. AirDrop transmits data via both Wi-Fi & Bluetooth, which you need to enable.

To send things with AirDrop

- Launch the item, then click ⬆, share, AirDrop, More options button•••, or another button that shows the application's sharing options.
- Click on the AirDrop icon◉, then click on the nearby AirDrop user profile picture.

To allow others to send things to your iPad via AirDrop

- Launch the control center, hold down the upper left set of controls, and click on the AirDrop icon◉.

- Then click on Contacts or Everybody to select those you want to get from.

  You can accept or reject each request.

Set DND

DND mute alerts & calls, and stops the screen from flashing

To activate DND

- Launch the Control Center and then click on the DND button ☽ to activate DND mode.

  When DND is active, the DND icon ☽ shows up in the menu bar.

- To select the end time of DND, hold down the DND icon ☽ in the Control Center, and then select one of the options like "1 hour" or "Till this event ends ".

  You can also click on Schedule, activate Scheduled, and choose start and end times.

Take a screenshot

- Press the top and volume up keys at the same time and release.

- Click on the screen shot in the bottom left part of your display, then click on Done, or click on full page
- Select Save

Record your screen

You can record your screen and capture the sound on your device.

- Enter the Setting application> Control Centre, then click ⊕ beside Screen Recording.
- Launch the Control Centre, click the Screen Record button⊙, and then wait for 3 seconds before the recording starts.
- When you are done and want to stop recording, launch the Control Center, click on the stop record button ⊙ , and then click on Stop.

Enter the photo application, and choose your video.

CHAPTER 3

MOVE DATA FROM AN OLD IPAD TO A NEW IPAD

We're all excited to get our hands on the latest iPad, but before we start using it with iPadOS 14; we need to make sure we've transferred all of our essential data to our new, greatest iPad. Otherwise, we have to start everything from the beginning and it will be a complete pain. Thankfully, Apple simplifies the process of transferring data to the new iPad. These are all you need to know about moving your data.

Make Use of the Automatic Setup feature

Any existing device can be used to set up a new iPad on iOS 11 and later when your current device and your new device are physically nearby, just by moving the settings from your current device to your new device.

1. With your new and current devices in immediate contact, choose your **language** on your new iPad.

2. Click **Continue** on the pop-up prompting you to set up your new iPad using your Apple ID.

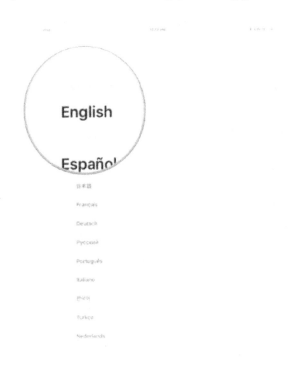

3. Scan the picture that displays on your new iPad with your old iPad.

4. On your new iPad, enter your old iPad **pin**.

5. Activate **Touch ID** On your new iPad.

6. Decide on whether or not to restore your **new iPad** from your former custom backup if this option shows up.

7. You will have to decide if you want to restore your **new device** from an iCloud or iTunes backup, set it up from scratch, or move data from an Android smartphone.

8. Agree to the terms and conditions.

9. Press **Continue** below **Express Settings** so you can use Siri's settings, Find My iPhone, Location, and use analytics moved from your former iPad.

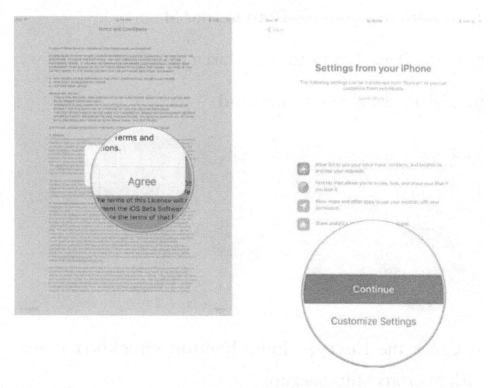

10. Now it's only a matter of finishing the iPad setup.

Use a Mac

macOS Catalina and later versions no longer have the iTunes app. As an alternative, iTunes is now divided into three new apps: Music, TV, and Podcasts. These apps don't have support for backing up, updating or restoring iPhones and iPads on Mac. For these tasks, you need to return to the Finder.

1. To start, link your old **iPad** to your Mac.

2. In the Dock, tap **Finder** to start a new Finder window.

3. Click the sidebar on your **iPad**.

4. Check the **Encrypt local backup checkbox** if you wish to protect this backup.

5. If you choose to encrypt your backups, enter a **password**.

6. Press the **Back Up Now** button. After doing it, be patient for the backup to finish before disconnecting your old iPad.

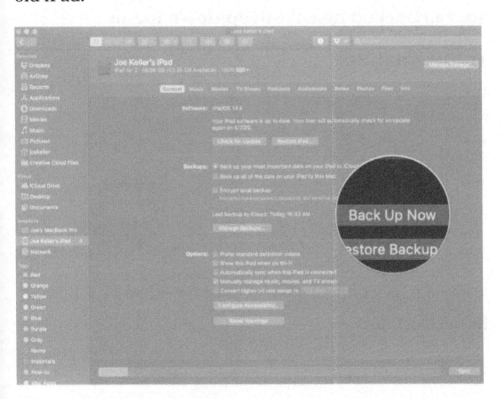

7. Now link your new **iPad** to the Mac which was used to back up your old iPad.

8. In the sidebar, choose your new **iPad**.

9. Select the **button** next to the **Restore from this backup** option from the drop-down menu.

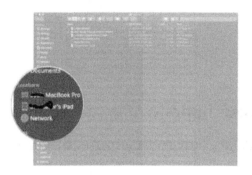 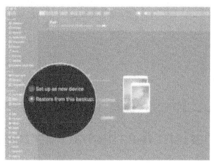

10. Tap **Backup** from the **drop-down menu**.

11. Tick **Continue**.

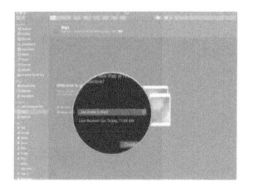 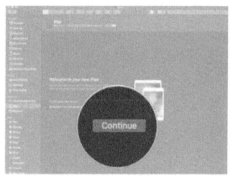

Complete the configuration of your new iPad by following the instructions.

Make use of iCloud

You can transfer everything to your new iPad wirelessly if iCloud was used to back up your iPad. But, before you do so, you should first enable the last physical backup on your old iPad to be sure that everything on your new device is as good as new.

1. Go to the **Settings** app on your old iPad.

2. Click on the **Apple ID banner**.

3. Click on **iCloud**.

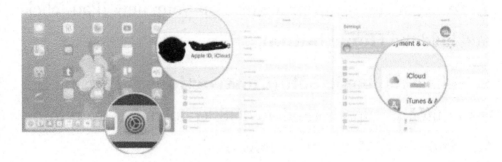

4. Click on **iCloud Backup**.

5. Press **Backup Now**.

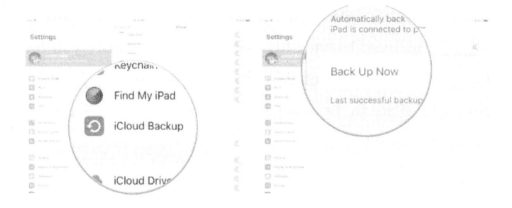

You'll want to begin using your new iPad after backing up your old one, and then recover the backup of the old one.

1. To begin the setup procedure on your new iPad, click and hold the **Home button**.

2. Follow the **basic setup instructions**. Try using the Automatic Setup method in iOS 11 to move everything from your old iPad to your new iPad.

3. Select **Restore from [the most recent backup date]**. When using Automatic Setup, backup to restore your most current iCloud backup.

4. Click **Agree**.

5. Complete your new iPad setup, including Siri, Location, App Analytics, and Apple Pay.

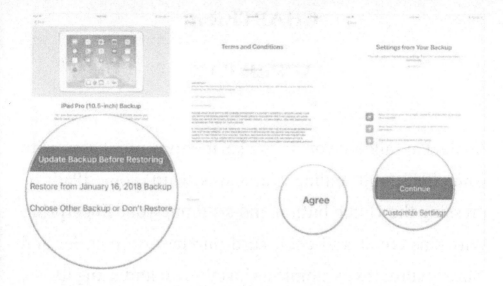

Your iPad will now be restored from your iCloud backup.
This may take some time.

CHAPTER 4

APPLE PAY

Apple Pay allows you to make in-store purchases with your iPad and online purchases with your iPad by pressing the Home button and scanning your fingerprint. With this credit and debit card purchases are easier and more secure. It's as simple as installing it and using it!

Adding Card to Apple Pay

1. From your Home screen, open the **Wallet app**.

2. Press down the **+ key**. Which is sited in the upper right corner of your screen.

3. Click on **Next** on the Apple Pay screen.

4. Manually enter or scan your **credit or debit card details.**

5. Press **Next** on the Card Details that appear on the screen.

6. Manually enter the **expiration date** and **security code** of the card.

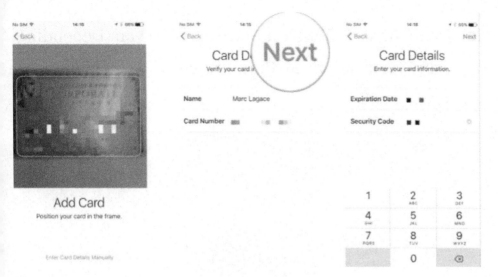

7. Press the **Next** button.

8. To accept the terms and conditions.

9. Press **Agree**.

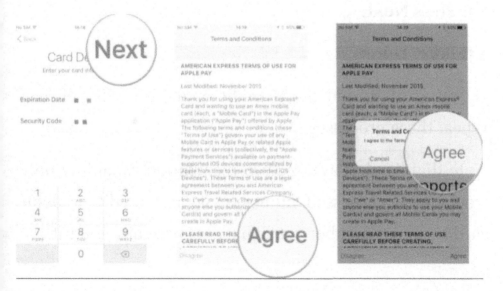

10. After selecting your verification method, click **Next**.

11. Press **Enter Code**.

12. Enter the **verification code** given to you. Depending on your verification method, it could be email, text message, or call.

13. Press **Next.**

14. Press **Done.**

If you want to add more credit or debit cards you can repeat these processes.

Note that Apple Pay's picture recognition capability only works with embossed numbers; if your credit or debit card has a flat number, you'll have to manually enter it.

Approve a Card for Apple Pay

Different banks do not have the same authentication methods for Apple Pay cards.

After you agree to your terms and conditions, Capital One will immediately add and activate your card for Apple Pay.

Citibank and American Express, on the other hand, require an activation code; to obtain one, the bank will automatically call, email, or text the phone number on file.

Moreover, if there is a mobile banking app from your bank, you can use it to authorize your card.

Change Your Apple Pay Default Card

You can use several credit and debit cards with Apple Pay and swap between them quickly anytime you want to make payments. A default credit or debit card, on the other hand, is often quicker and easier to use. So you'd like to set that card as the default. Fortunately, Apple Pay has made it possible to be quick and easy.

1. Open the Apple Pay custom **Settings app** on your iPad.

2. Press **Wallet & Apple Pay**.

3. Click on **Default Card**.

4. Click on the card you want to use by default.

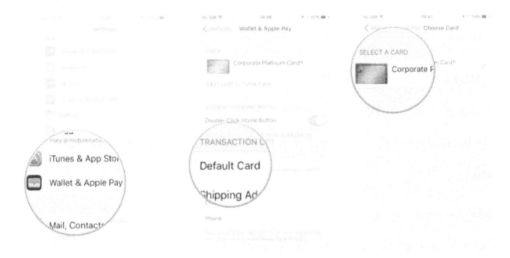

So much! The selected card will always be used unless you manually change the card you used to purchase.

Delete an Apple Pay Card

Apple Pay makes it simple to enroll all of your compatible credit and debit cards. However, if you lose, cancel or substitute the card for any motive, you must eliminate the card. Fortunately, Apple is making it easier.

1. Launch the **Settings** app on your iPad, and find the Apple Pay card you want to delete.

2. Select **Wallet & Apple** Pay from the drop-down menu.

3. Delete the **credit card** by tapping it.

4. Slide to the bottom and click **Remove This Card.**

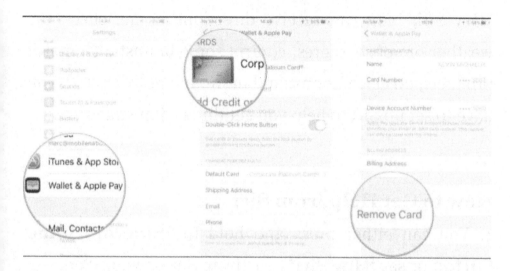

That concludes the procedure. The removed card is no longer qualified for use with Apple Pay on that device. Apple Pay, on the other hand, operates per device, meaning you'll need to remove the card from each linked device separately. Alternatively, you can remove all your linked cards remotely from the specified device via iCloud.com if needed.

CHAPTER 5

SIRI

You can use Siri, Apple's virtual, personal, and digital assistant if you have the greatest iPad. With you saying "Hey Siri," you can receive directions home, check the weather or sports scores, control some fantastic HomeKit products, do calculations, and more. In another word, you have to set up Siri to help you get things done quicker.

How to Get Help from Siri

1. You can either press and hold the **Side or Home button** or say **'Hey Siri'** to activate Siri on your iPad.

2. Begin by uttering your command or query.

How to Use the Settings App to Activate and Deactivate Siri

When you initially set up your iPad, iOS frequently asks if you want to enable Siri. If Siri isn't already enabled, you can always turn it on from Settings. The same thing happens to stop it.

1. Enter the **Settings app** on your iPad.

2. Move down and click **Siri & Search**.

3. Tap the **button** next to Listen for "Hey Siri" to launch Hey Siri.

4. To activate Siri accesses through the Side or Home button toggle the button succeeding to **Press Side/Home button for Siri**.

5. To reach Siri when your iPad is locked, press the **button** next to **Allow Siri when locked**.

"Hey Siri": How to Set It Up

Do you want Siri to answer even if you haven't pressed the Home button? Activate "Hey Siri", which allows you to say an anonymous slogan to activate your iPad assistant.

1. Open the **Settings** on your iPad.

2. Go down and press **Siri & Search**.

3. Choose the switch next to **Listen for "Hey Siri"** and switch it on. If "Hey Siri" is on, the switch turns green.

4. Press the **Continue** button.

5. Follow the **on-screen directions**.

6. Click the **Done** button.

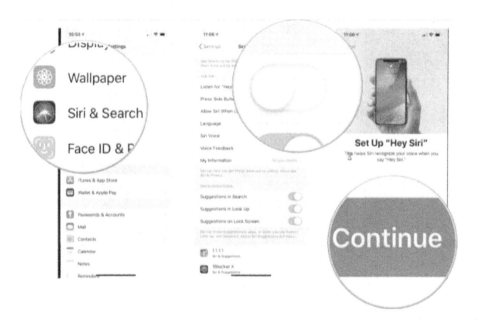

Change Siri's tone of voice

You may alter Siri's voice if you don't like it or prefer an accent that sounds similar to your own.

1. Open the **Settings** on your iPad.

2. Click on **Siri & Search**.

3. Choose a **Siri Voice** from the Siri menu.

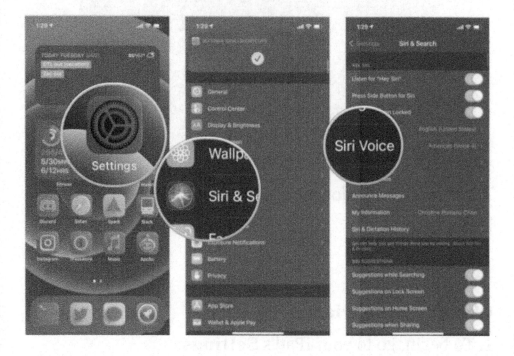

4. Pick from one of the following **accents**: American, Australian, British, Indian, Irish, or South African.

5. Tap the **voice style** you like. There are four tones.

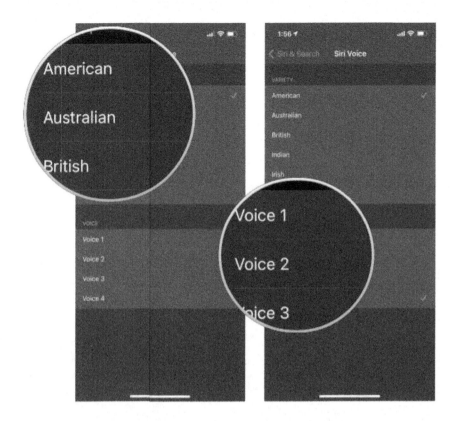

The voice will be downloaded if you don't have it on your iPad.

Change Siri's Dialect

1. To begin, go to your iPad's **Settings**.

2. Tick **Siri & Search**.

3. Touch **Language**.

4. Pick the **language** of your choice.

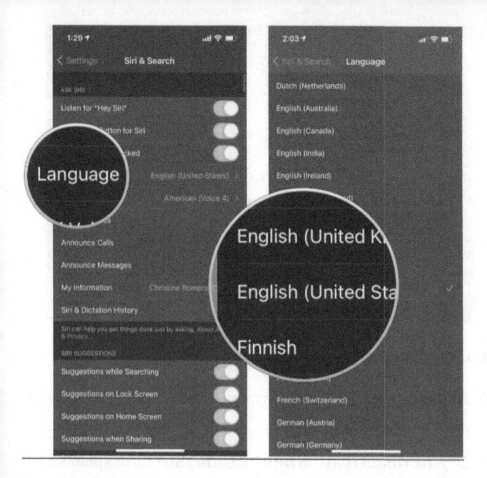

How to Make Siri's Responses Customized

1. Open the **Settings** on your iPad.

2. Click on **Siri & Search.**

3. Select **Siri Responses**.

4. Choose an **option**:

❖ **Always on**: Siri can always hear you whether your iPad is on silent or not.

❖ **If you deactivate Silent Mode**, Siri only speaks out when you say "Hey Siri," or when it is connected to a Bluetooth device or CarPlay.

❖ **Only when you say "Hey Siri"** or when you're linked to a Bluetooth device or CarPlay will Siri answer vocally.

5. Click on the **toggle** if you want to **Always Show Siri Captions**.

6. If you want to **Always Show Speech** transliteration, tap the **toggle** button.

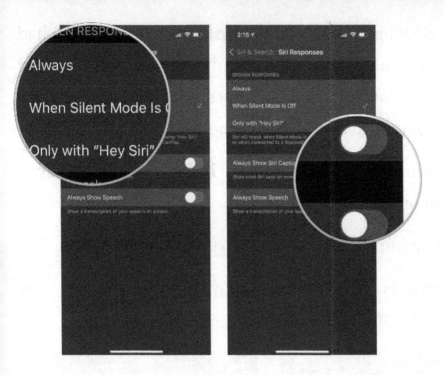

How to Make Changes to a Siri Command or Inquiry

You can acquire full transcripts of your query or allow you to change them by putting an order for Siri if you always turn on **Always Show Speech** from **Siri Responses**. This is helpful if Siri doesn't understand what you are saying or if you only want to tweak a few words rather than repeating the entire conversation.

If you don't have the Always Show Speech option turned on, this won't function. Always Show Siri Captions isn't required, but it may be quite useful if you want to know precisely what Siri is saying. Earlier versions of iOS had this by default, but in iOS 14 and later, Apple has moved to a more Compact User Interface, so you need to enable transcriptions to edit your Siri queries.

1. To launch Siri, **press and hold the Side/Home button** or utter **"Hey Siri."**

2. Ask an inquiry or provide instruction.

3. At the bottom of the display, tap the **text** of your request or command.

4. Make any necessary **changes** to your text.

5. Click the **Done** button. Your updated query or command will now be answered by Siri.

How to Modify Siri's Contact Data

Siri uses your contact card information to do tasks like "give me routes home" or "call my mom." If you've changed cards or want Siri to focus on other information, you may change Siri's settings.

1. Enter the **Settings** app on your iPad.

2. Move to the bottom and press **Siri & Search**.

3. Click **My Info**.

4. Tap the **contact** information that Siri wants to use. You must generate a contact for yourself if you wish to use it.

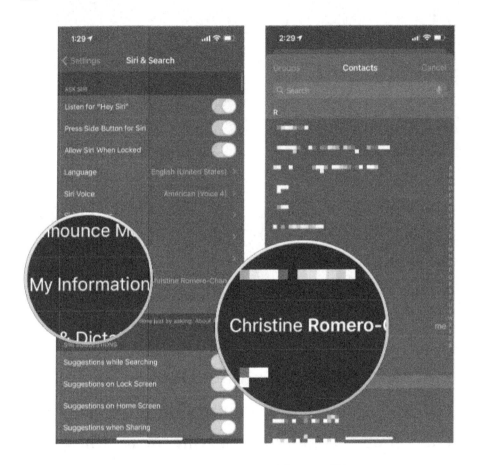

If you want Siri to do things like calling your mom or significant other, you first need to make sure you have established relationships with your contacts.

How to Encrypt Siri Using a Passcode

Because Siri is generally enabled by just holding down the Home button, it can put your iPhone or iPad's data at risk. If you're disturbed about security and have a Passcode Lock on your iPhone or iPad, make sure Siri isn't permitted to bypass it – it'll be problematic, but that's always the worth of the security.

1. Begin by going to the **Settings** app on your iPad.

2. Click on **Touch ID & Passcode.**

3. Type your **password**.

4. Move to the bottom to the **Allow access when locked** section and press **Siri** to turn off the capability to use Siri when your iPad is locked.

How to Set Up the iPad's Default Settings

1. To activate Siri, press down the **Side/Home button** on your iPad or speak **"Hey Siri."**

2. Say things like **Turn off my screen brightness, Turn off Wi-Fi,** or **Turn on Airplane Mode.**

3. Wait for Siri to comprehend what you've said before disabling or enabling the desired setting.

CHAPTER 6

HOW TO CONNECT YOUR IPAD TO THE INTERNET WITH WI-FI

This manual tells you how to connect your iPad to Wi-Fi, whether it's a public or password-protected private network.

Connecting an iPad to the Internet via Wi-Fi

Follow these instructions to connect your iPad to Wi-Fi when you wish to go online:

1. Tap **Settings** from the iPad's home screen.

2. Select **Wi-Fi**.

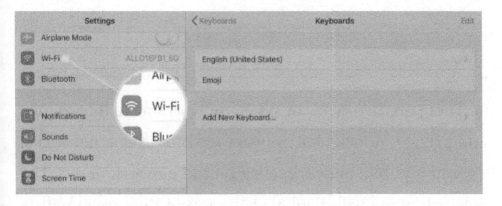

3. Move the **Wi-Fi** slider to on/green to start the iPad looking for local wireless networks. A list of all nearby networks will appear after some seconds. There are indicators next to each one indicating whether it's public or private, as well as the strength of the signal.

Note that if you don't see any networks, none may be within range.

4. There are two types of Wi-Fi networks available: public and private. A lock icon appears next to private networks. To join a public network, click on the network name. The network name will display at the top of the screen with a tick next to it if your iPad was permitted to connect to the network.

Note: There is a three-line Wi-Fi indicator that displays next to each network name, showing the network's signal strength. The stronger the signal, the blacker bars there are in that icon. Join a network that has more bars wherever possible. They'll be more convenient to connect to and provide a speedier connection.

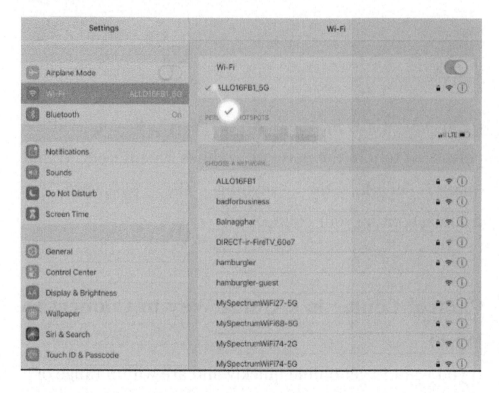

5. A password is required to get access to a private network. In the pop-up box, tap the network name and input the password. Tap the **Join** button, which appears on the pop-up menu.

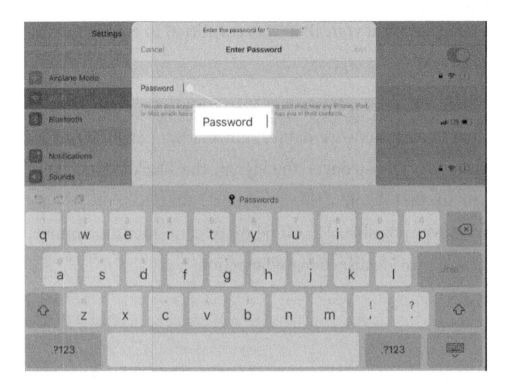

6. If you type in the correct password you will be permitted to join the network and use the internet. If that doesn't work, try retyping the password or troubleshooting your connection.

Control Center is a Quick Way to Connect to Wi-Fi

If you want to get online quickly and are within range of a network you've already connected to (for example, at home or work), you can use Control Center to instantly turn on Wi-Fi. For this to happen, slide down from the top-right corner of the screen. Tap the Wi-Fi symbol in Control Center to make it stand out. Any local Wi-Fi network to which your iPad has previously connected will be used.

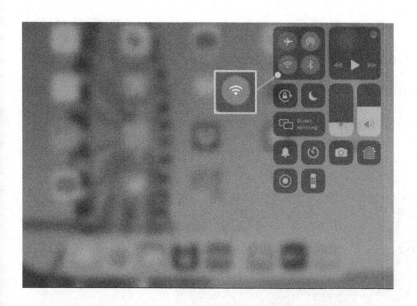

Wi-Fi Hotspots and Data Security

While it's fantastic to find a free, open Wi-Fi network when you need one, you should equally be concerned about security. Connecting to a Wi-Fi network you've never used before and aren't convinced you can trust might leave your online activity vulnerable to monitoring or hacking. Checking your bank account or making transactions via an insecure Wi-Fi network are both bad ideas. When connecting to a Wi-Fi hotspot, be mindful of the things to check for.

CHAPTER 7

CAMERA

Learn how to use the Camera app on your iPad to take excellent images. Choose from a variety of camera settings, including Photo, Pano, and Square, as well as features like Burst and Live Photos.

Take a Picture

When you first start the Camera, the default mode is Photo. To snap still photos, switch to Photo mode. Toggle between Video, Pano, Time-lapse, Slo-mo, and Portrait modes by swiping up or down on the mode selection.

1. To launch the Camera in Photo mode, open the Camera or slide left on the Lock screen on the Home screen.

2. To capture the photo, press the Shutter button or either volume button.

Press the Flash button and select Auto, on, or off on devices that have support for True Tone Flash or Retina Flash.

Set a timer and compose your shot while stabilizing your iPad. Tap the Timer button, and then select 3s or 10s from the drop-down menu.

Note: When the camera is in use, a green dot displays at the top of the screen for your safety.

Make a panoramic photograph

1. Select Pano mode, then press and hold the Shutter button.

2. Slowly pan in the arrow's direction while staying on the centerline.

3. To finish, press the Shutter button once more.

To move the camera in the other way, click on the arrow. Pan vertically by turning iPad to landscape mode. A vertical pan can also be reversed in direction.

Take a Selfie

1. Click the back-facing camera symbol or the back-facing camera icon to go to the front camera (Depending on your model).

2. Make sure the iPad is facing you.

3. To take a photo either taps the Shutter button or any of the volume buttons.

Taking Selfie in Portrait Mode

You may use the front camera to add a depth-of-field effect to your selfies on compatible devices. This technique maintains your face distinct while blurring the surroundings attractively.

1. Select the Portrait mode.

The front-facing camera is now operational.

2. In the yellow portrait box, you can frame yourself.

3. Click the Shutter button to take the photo.

Alter Lighting in Portrait Mode Selfies

The studio-quality lighting effects in Portrait mode selfies can be used on devices that have Portrait Lighting.

1. Select Portrait mode before framing your selfie.

2. To select a lighting effect, drag the Portrait Lighting control:

* ❖ **Natural Light:** Against a hazy background, the face is sharply focused.
* ❖ **Studio Lighting:** The face is nicely lighted, and the shot appears to be clean overall.
* ❖ **Contour Light:** There are dramatic shadows on the face, as well as highlights and lowlights.
* ❖ **Stage Light** makes the face spotlit against a black background.
* ❖ **Stage Light Mono** has a similar effect with Stage Light, except that it has a shot in black and white.

3. Click on the Shutter button to capture the photo.

Alter the Depth Control in Selfies in Portrait Mode

The Depth Control slider can be used to alter the degree of background blur in your Portrait mode selfies on models that have supported it.

1. Select Portrait mode before framing your selfie.

2. On the right side of the screen tick the Depth Adjustment button. The Depth Control slider is found on the right side of the screen.

3. To change the effect, move the slider up or down.

4. Click on the Shutter button to snap the photo.

The Depth Control slider in Photos can be used to adjust the background blur effect, after recording in Portrait mode.

How to Capture Action Images with Burst Mode

Burst mode shoots a series of high-speed shots, giving you a variety of images to pick from. Burst shots can be captured with both the front and back cameras.

1. Pick either from Photo or Square mode.

2. To capture rapid-fire pictures press down the Shutter button. The counter displays the number of shots you've taken.

3. Stop by lifting your finger.

4. Tap the Burst thumbnail, then tap **Select** to select the photographs you wish to preserve. The suggested photos are indicated by gray dots beneath the thumbnails.

5. To save each photo as an individual photo, hit the circle in the lower-right corner, then tap Done. To remove the whole group of Burst photographs, touch the thumbnail, then the Delete button.

Take a Real-Time Photo

A Live Photo captures all of the events that occur before, during, and after you shoot your photo, even audio.

1. Choose Photo mode on devices that allow Live Photos.

2. By clicking the Live Photo button, you can turn Live Photos on (yellow is on) or off.

3. Tap on the Shutter icon to snap the image.

Live Photos are labeled "Live" in the top-left corner of your albums. Live Photos can be edited and added effects like Loop and Bounce.

Shoot Videos with Your iPad's Camera

You can use a camera to shoot videos and switch between modes to record slow-motion and time-lapse footage on your iPad.

Create a Video

1. Tick on the Video option.

2. To begin recording, hit the Record button or either volume button. To zoom in or out, try pinching the screen.

3. To stop recording, hit the Record button or either volume button.

Video is shot at 30 frames per second (frames per second) by default. Depending on your model, you can alter the frame rate and video resolution by going to **Settings > Camera > Record Video**. Larger video files result from higher frame rates and resolutions.

Note: When the camera is in use, a green dot displays at the top of the screen for your safety.

Alter The Video Resolution and Frame Rate with The Quick Toggles.

You can alter the video resolution and frame rate available on your iPad in Video mode by using the quick switches at the top of the screen. You can find the quick toggles, by going to Settings > Camera > Record Video, then turn on Video Format Control.

Take a Video in Slow Motion

1. Select slo-mo mode.

2. Click the Record button or either volume button to begin and end shooting.

Tap the video thumbnail, and then tap Edit, to make a portion of it play in slow motion while the rest plays normally. Drag the vertical bars below the frame viewer to identify the portion you wish to replay in slow motion.

You can vary the frame rate and resolution depending on your model. The resultant video file grows in size as the frame rate and resolution increase.

Go to Settings > Camera > Record Slo-mo to adjust the Slo-mo recording settings.

Make a Time-Lapse Video

1. Select the Time-lapse option.

2. Set up your iPad at a location where you wish to capture a sunset, traffic flow, or another event over time.

3. To begin recording the video, click on the Record icon; to stop recording the video, click on the Record icon again.

iPad Allows You to View, Share, And Print Images

Photos save all of the photos and videos you take with the camera. All new images and videos are automatically uploaded and made accessible in Photos on all of your iCloud Photos-enabled devices when you activate iCloud Photos (with iOS 8.1, iPadOS 13, or later).

Note: If the Settings > Privacy Location Services is activated, the location data for photos and videos can be used by applications and platforms of photo-sharing.

Look At Your Photos

1. Tap the thumbnail image below the Shutter button in the Camera.

2. Swipe right to see the most recent photos you've shot. If you want to show or hide the controls, click on the screen.

3. To see all of your photos and videos saved in Photos, tap All Photos.

You Can Share and Print Photos

1. When looking at an image, press the Share button.

2. Select a sharing method, such as AirDrop, Mail, or Messages, to send your picture.

3. To print your photo, swipe up from the list of options and pick Print from the drop-down menu.

How to Upload and Sync Photos across Several Devices

iCloud Images allows you to upload photos and videos from your iPad to iCloud and access them from any iPhone, iPad, or iPod touch with the same Apple ID. If you want to keep your images up to date across several devices or save space on your iPad, iCloud Photo is a good option. To activate iCloud Photos, go to Settings > Photos. Even if iCloud Photos is turned off, you can still preserve up to 1000 of your most current pictures in the My Photo Stream album on iCloud-connected devices.

Scanning QR Code with the iPad Camera

You can Scan QR codes for links to websites, apps, coupons, tickets, and more with the Camera or the Code Scanner. A QR code is immediately detected and highlighted by the camera.

Read a QR Code with the Camera

1. Position the iPad such that the code appears on the screen after opening the Camera.

2. To proceed to the relevant website or app, tap the notification that displays on the screen.

From the Control Center, Enter the Code Scanner

1. Tap the Insert button next to Code Scanner in Settings > Control Center.

2. Open Control Center, touch Code Scanner, and then move iPad so the code displays on the screen.

3. To turn on the flashlight, tap it to turn it on.

CHAPTER 8

ICLOUD

Apple's document and file management solution for iPhone, iPad and Mac is iCloud Drive. If you do have an iCloud account, you can access iCloud Drive.

You'll get 5GB of free storage by default, but you may upgrade your capacity with a monthly subscription. Depending on your storage demands, subscriptions range from free to $9.99 per month.

If you're not sure where to begin, this guide will walk you through the setup process and show you how to use iCloud Drive right now!

Activating iCloud Drive on an iPad Manually

When you initially set up your iPad, you should be asked if you want to use iCloud Drive. If you responded yes, you don't need to do anything further and can continue to the next section. If you said no, iCloud Drive can be enabled with only a few touches.

1. Open the **Settings** application.

2. Press the **Apple ID banner**.

3. Select **iCloud** from the menu.

4. Scroll down and tap the **iCloud Drive On/Off** button.

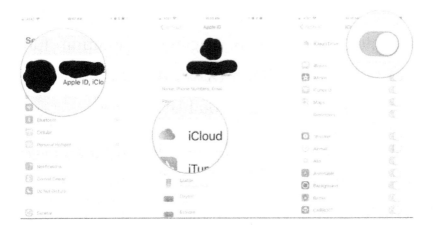

Remember that if you turn off iCloud Drive, you won't be able to save anything until you re-enable it.

How to Expand the Storage Capacity of iCloud Drive on an iPad

iCloud Drive comes with 5GB of free storage by default. You can subscribe to a larger storage plan if you feel this isn't sufficient. If you currently have an iCloud subscription, you can make changes to it to better fit your immediate requirements.

1. Open the **Settings** application.

2. Press the **Apple ID banner**.

3. From the menu, choose **iCloud**.

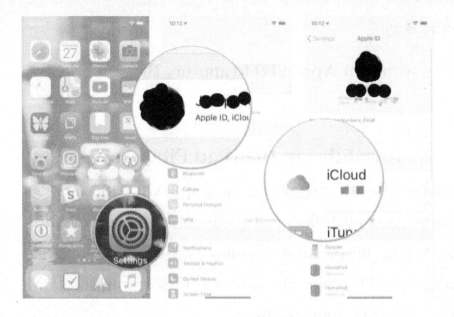

4. From the menu, choose **Manage Storage**.

5. Choose **Change Storage Plan** from the menu that appears.

6. Choose the **storage plan** that best meets your requirements.

7. Select **Buy**.

8. Login with your **Apple ID** to approve the purchase.

How to Move Files in the iPad Files App

You'll find iCloud Drive in the Files app. On iOS, the Files app offers a multitude of storage and file organization options. You don't have to use app-based folders to organize your files; you may use the Files app in the same way you would Dropbox or Box.

1. To get started, go to the **Files** app.

2. Choose **Browse** at the end of the page.

3. Click **iCloud Drive** under the **Locations section**.

4. To launch a **folder,** click it.

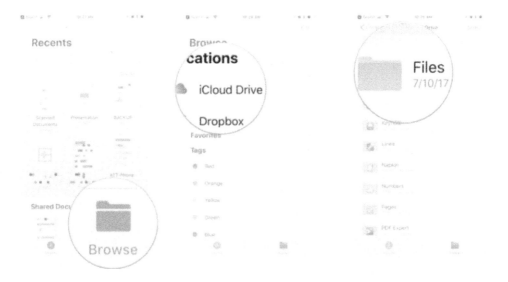

5. Tap **Select** in the screen's upper right corner.

6. Tap on the **files** you wish to transfer to make a selection.

7. At the end of the screen, click on **Move**.

8. To choose a location for the files, tap a **folder**.

9. In the topmost right corner of the screen, hit **Move**.

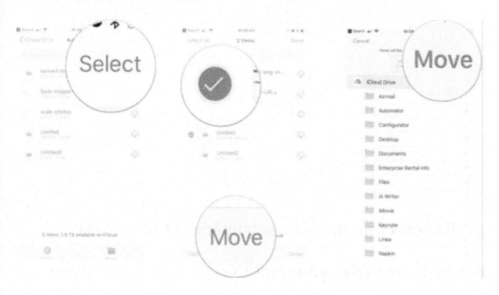

How to Delete Files from the iPad Files App

You may fluently delete files that you no longer need if you run out of space or simply wish to tidy.

1. Launch the **Files** app.

2. Choose **Browse** at the end of the screen.

3. In the **Locations** section, tap **iCloud Drive**.

4. To launch a **folder**, click it.

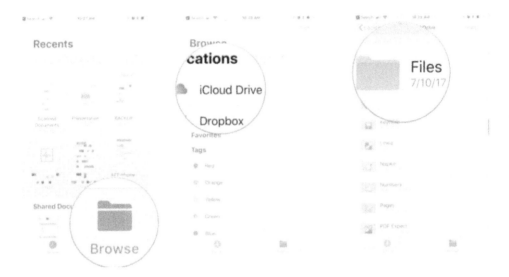

5. Hit **Select** on the upper-right edge of the screen.

6. Choose the **files** you want to erase by clicking them.

7. In the bottom right-hand corner, tap **Delete**. (Note: There is no confirmation process. The files will be marked for deletion when you delete them, but they can be recovered in the Files app's **Recently Deleted** folder).

How to Enable or Disable Cellular Data for Files App Syncing

If you have a lot of documents in the Files app and have a restricted data plan, you might want to disable cellular data usage for the app. Here's how to do it.

1. Open the **Settings** application.

2. Click on **Cellular**.

3. Scroll down until you find the **Files** app in the **Cellular Data** area.

4. Toggle cellular data use off by tapping the **On/Off** switch.

This will ensure that iCloud Drive does not consume any cell data. Save your cash!

CHAPTER 9

SAFARI

With the Safari app, you can surf the web, save webpages to your reading list for later reading, and add page icons to your Home Screen for easy access. If the Apple ID you use to log in to your iCloud account on all of your devices is the same, you can see all sites that were opened on the other devices and keep your bookmarks, history, and reading queue updated.

See your bookmarks, reading list, and shared links.

Enter a web address, do a search, or quickly access your favorites.

View open tabs.

Open a new tab.

Share, print, and more.

Browse the Web with Safari

With just a few clicks, you can simply navigate a webpage.

❖ ***Return to the top:*** To go back quickly to the start of a long page double-tap the screen's top border.

❖ Position the iPad in landscape mode to ***view more of the page***.

❖ ***Reload the page*** by touching the Reload button close to the address in the search field.

❖ ***Share the following links***: Click the "Share" button.

Amend Display, Text Size, and Website Settings

Safari for iPad presents the desktop version of a webpage, which is intelligently resized for the iPad display and optimized for touch input.

The View menu lets you alter the font size, change to Reader view, generate privacy restrictions, and more.

To access the View menu, click the Website Options button on the left side of the search box, and then select one of the options below:

- ❖ *Increase or decrease the text size*: To increase or reduce the text size, tap the large A or the small A.

- ❖ *View the page without any advertisements or menus*: Toggle the Show Reader View switch on (if available).

- ❖ To conceal the toolbar, click Hide toolbar (To get it back, click the top of the screen.)

- ❖ *Set your display and privacy preferences for each visit to this website*: Go to Website Settings and select it.

Split View Allows You to See Two Pages Side by Side

Use Split View to launch two Safari pages side by side.

- ❖ *In Split View, start with a blank page*: To open a new window, press and hold the Pages button.

- ❖ *Access link in Split View*: Hold the link with your hand, then click Open in New Window.

- ❖ *Flip a window to the Split View's other side*: Drag left or right after touching and holding the top of the window.

- ❖ *To close tabs in a Split View window, do the following*: Keep your finger on the Pages button.

- ❖ To **exit Split View**, slide the divider over the window you choose to close.

You Can Make Translation for a Website

(Beta) You can use Safari to translate a text on a webpage that is written in another language.

Tap the Website Options button, then the Translate button when reading a webpage in a different language.

Take Advantage of Keyboard Shortcuts

An external keyboard can be used to navigate Safari using keyboard shortcuts.

To view the keyboard shortcuts that are available, press and hold the Command key.

Safari on iPad allows you to look for Websites

Enter a URL or a search query in the Safari app to find websites or specialized information.

Use the Internet to Look Up Information

1. Input a search term, phrase, or URL into the search field at the top of the screen.

2. To find exactly what you typed, tap a search suggestion or press Go on the keyboard.

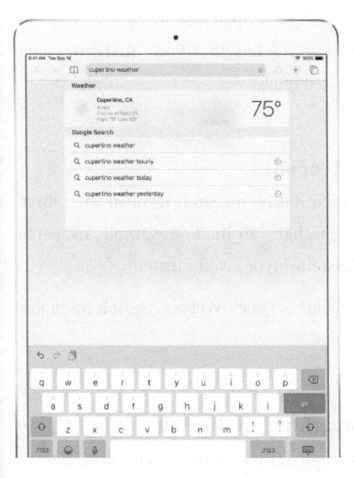

If you don't want to see suggested search keywords you can go to Settings > Safari > Search Engine Suggestions to switch it off.

Look for Websites you've previously visited

Your open tabs, bookmarks, and recently viewed pages are all included in Safari's search suggestions. If you search for "iPad," for example, the search options under Switch to Tab cover all your open tabs linked to "iPad," as well as websites interrelated to "iPad" that you have bookmarked or visited lately.

Search Inside Websites

Enter a website followed by a search term in the search area to search within that website. For example, to search Wikipedia for "Einstein," type "wiki Einstein."

Go to Settings > Safari > Quick Website Search to enable or disable this option.

Search for Something on the Page

On a page, you can look for a certain word or phrase.

1. After tapping the Share icon, select Find on Page.

2. Input the keyword you're searching for in the search field.

3. To locate more examples, press the Search Down button.

Select a Search Engine

Enter Safari > Settings > Search Engine.

Safari On iPad allows you to Block Advertisements and Other Distractions

Use Safari Reader to browse a page without advertisements, navigation menus, or other distracting features in the Safari app.

Tap to view the page in reader.

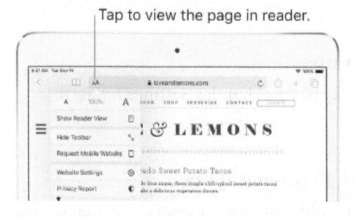

Display Reader's View

A webpage is formatted in Reader view to show only the necessary information and images.

At the left end of the address box, tap the Format Options button, then click on Show Reader View.

Tap the Format Options button, then Hide Reader View to return to the entire page.

Note: Reader view is not visible for that page if the Format Options button is darkened.

For A Webpage, Use Reader View by Default

1. Tap the Format Options button, then Website Settings on a supported website.

2. Use Reader Automatically should be turned on.

Disabled Pop-ups

Block Pop-ups may be found under Settings > Safari.

Check Out the Privacy Report

Safari makes it difficult for trackers to follow you throughout the internet. You can see a list of cookies that Intelligent Tracking Prevention has found and disabled on the actual webpage you're browsing in the Privacy Report. You can also check and change Safari configurations to maintain your browsing activity secret and to protect against harmful sites.

To access the Privacy Report, go to the left side of the search field and press the Website Options button, then Privacy Report.

How Control Privacy and Security Settings for Safari

Turn on or off any of the following scenarios under Privacy & Security in Settings > Safari:

1. Avoid Cross-Site Tracking: Safari blocks third-party trackers and data by default. Turn this setting off if you don't want cross-site tracking.

2. Turn on Block All Cookies to prevent websites from placing cookies on your iPad. (To clear cookies that have already been installed on your iPad, go to Settings > Safari > Clear History and Website Data.)

3. If you visit a suspected phishing website, Safari will display a warning. Turn this option off if you wouldn't like to be alerted about fake websites.

4. Check for Apple Pay: Websites that accept Apple Pay can see if you have the service enabled on your device.

To stop websites from verifying if you have Apple Pay, turn this option off.

When you use Safari to browse a non-secure website, a warning shows in the Safari search field.

Delete Your Surfing History and Website Data

History and website data can be removed from your history by going into Safari's settings and selecting "Clear History & Website Data."

Visit Historical Sites without Making Any History

Select Private from the Pages menu.

When Private Browsing Mode is on, the Safari theme is black rather than white, and the pages you surf don't display in your iPad's History or the list of tabs on your other devices.

To hide the websites and quit Private Browsing Mode, press the Pages button, and then touch Private once more. When you use Private Browsing Mode again, the sites reappear.

CHAPTER 10

MAIL

Make up an Email in iPad Mail

Using the iPad Mail app, you can write and edit emails, as well as send or receive images, videos, sketches, files, and more.

Change mailboxes or accounts.

Delete, move, or mark multiple messages.

Compose a message.

Make a Message for Email

Inquire of Siri. "New email to Kevin Bishop," for example, or "Email Joel and say I received the forms, thanks." Alternatively, try the following:

1. To begin, use the **Compose button**.

2. After tapping in the email, type your message.

On the display keyboard, you can click single keys. By pinching closed and swiping your finger through one letter to the next without withdrawing your finger, you can use the tiny QuickType keyboard.

3. Tap the Text Styles button to adjust the formatting.

You can alter the font style, text color, bold or italic style; add a bulleted or numbered list, and much more.

Response to an Email

1. Tap the email, then the Reply button, and finally Reply.

2. Type your response in the box.

On the display keyboard, you can click single keys. By pinching closed and swiping your finger through one letter to the next without withdrawing your finger, you can use the tiny QuickType keyboard.

An Email Can Have a Document Attached to It

You can send an email with a stored document attached.

1. Above the keyboard, press the Insert Attachment button in the email where you wish to upload the document.

2. In **Files**, find the document you want to insert and tap it.

If you want to access a file, location, or folder in Files press Browse or Recent at the bottom of the screen. You can also slide a file into an email to add it.

Add a Picture or Video which you've stored earlier

1. Click the Insert Photo Toolbar button in the email where you want to upload the photo or video, and then touch the Take Photo or Video Toolbar button above the keyboard.

2. In the photo selector, look for the photo or video. You can see more photographs by swiping up.

3. To add a photo or video to your email, tap on the photo or video.

Take a Picture or Record a Video to Include in an Email

1. Click the email where you wish to insert the photo or video, and then press the Camera Toolbar button above the keyboard.

2. Take a new image or video.

3. To insert it (photo or video) into your email, click Use Photo or Use Video, or click Retake if you wish to reshoot it.

Scanning Document and Attach It to An Email

1. To upload a scanned document to an email address, click the Scan Toolbar button above the keyboard.

2. Place the iPad so that the document page displays on the screen; the iPad will capture the page automatically. Press a volume button or click the Take Picture icon to manually capture the page. Toggle the flash on or off by tapping the Show Flash Settings button.

3. Scan more pages and then click Save when you're finished.

4. If you want to change a saved scan, click on it and then pick one of the choices below:

❖ *Crop the image as follows:* Select the Crop option.
❖ *Insert a filter to it:* From the drop-down box, pick Show Filter Settings.
❖ To flip the image, press the *Rotate button.*
❖ Delete the scan by clicking the Delete scan button.

You can make a Note of an Attachment

With Markup, you can scribble or sketch on a photo, video, or PDF file.

1. Tap the attachment in the email, and then turn off the Markup Switch button.

2. Use the drawing tools with your finger or Apple Pencil.

3. Once you're through, tap Done.

Create a Sketch of Your Email

1. Click the Markup button above the keyboard in the email where you wish to put a sketch.

2. Choose a color and a sketching tool, and then use your finger to write or draw.

3. Tap Done, then Insert Drawing after you're finished. Click the drawing in the email, and then click on the Markup button to continue work on it.

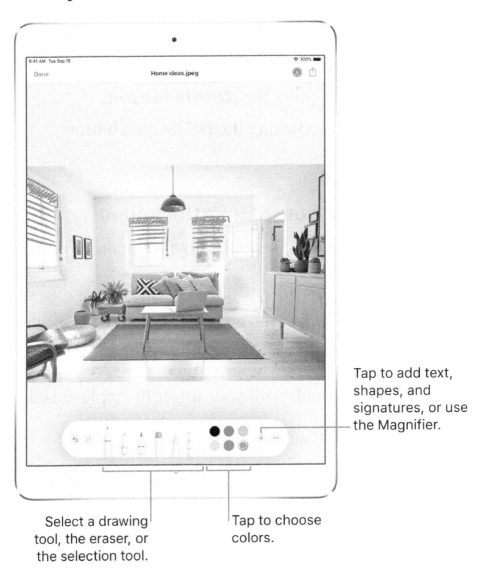

Tap to add text, shapes, and signatures, or use the Magnifier.

Select a drawing tool, the eraser, or the selection tool.

Tap to choose colors.

CHAPTER 11

NOTES

Use Your iPad to Take Notes

With checklists, photos, web connections, scanned documents, handwritten notes, and sketches, you may jot down brief thoughts or arrange complex information with the Notes app.

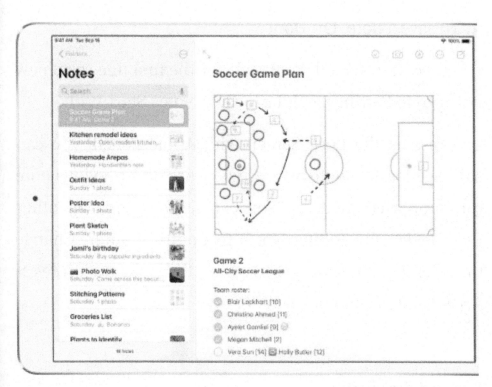

Make A New Note and Format It

Requesting "Make a fresh note" from Siri is possible.

Alternatively, try the following:

1. Tap the New Note button and type your message. The note's title is determined by the first line of the note.

2. To adjust the format, tap the Format button. There are options for a headline style, bold or italic font, a bulleted or numerical list, and more.

3. To save a note, tap Done.

If you want to set a default style for the first line in all new notes go to Settings > Notes > New Notes Start With.

By pressing the Lock Screen with Apple Pencil, you can easily generate a note or continue work on a previous note (on supported models). You can perform this on other iPad devices by adding Notes to Control Center. Change the Lock Screen settings, by going to Settings > Notes > Access Note from Lock Screen.

Use a Checklist

Tap the Checklist button in a note, and then perform one of the following:

- ❖ ***Add stuff to the list***: Tap return to move on to the next item after entering text.

- ❖ ***Indentation can be increased or decreased***: Swipe the object to the right or left.

- ❖ ***To specify that an item has been finalized add a checkmark:*** To add a checkmark; click the blank circle succeeding to the item.

- ❖ ***Reorder a product***: Drag the item to a new location in the list by touching and holding the empty circle or checkbox next to it.

- ❖ Click the list to launch the menu, and then touch the Show More Items button, and then pick Checklist, then Check All, Uncheck All, Delete Checked, or Move Checked to Bottom to ***manage the stuff in the list***.

Go to Settings > Notes > Sort Checked Items, then click automatically to sort checked items at the bottom of all your notes.

Change The Way Your iPad's Notes Are Displayed

- ❖ ***Fill the screen with the note:*** Tap the Enter Full-Screen button or rotate the iPad to portrait orientation while viewing a note in landscape mode.

❖ *At a glance, see your accounts, notes list, and selected note:* (12.9-inch iPad Pro) Tap the Show Sidebar button after adjusting the iPad to landscape mode.

You Can Look for and Organize Your Notes in Folders on iPad

You can look for all of your notes in the Notes app for typed and written text, stuffs in photos, and text in scanned documents. You can also put your notes in folders and pin the best vital ones to the top of the list.

You Can Create, Rename, Move, or Delete Folder or Subfolder

Do one of the following:

* *Make a folder:* Tap New Folder and give your folder a name.

* *Make a subfolder:* Drag a folder from one folder to another by touching and holding it.

* *Rename a folder:* Click a folder, then press the Folder Actions button, then click Rename and input a new name.

* *Transfer a folder:* Slide left on the folder, press the Move Folder button, and then pick a new location. Otherwise, press and hold the folder before sliding it to a new location. If you transfer the folder onto another folder, it becomes a subfolder.

* *Wipe away (delete) a folder:* Slide left on the folder, and then tick the Delete Folder button. Otherwise, you can press and hold the folder, then click on Delete.

If you have a change of heart, you can bring back the notes by going to the Recently Deleted folder.

Sort, Transfer, Pin, Delete or View Notes in Gallery View

In the list of notes, do one of the following:

❖ *Change the view of the folder:* Tap the Folder Actions button and select View as Gallery or View as List.

❖ *Amend the sort order of folders:* Click on the Folder Actions button, click on "Sort by" and select Date Edited, Date Created, or Title. To pick the default type procedure for all folders, enter Settings> Notes> Sort Notes By.

❖ *Transfer a note to another folder:* Swipe left on the note and press the Move Folder button. Or touch and hold a note, press Move, and select a folder.

❖ *PIN a vital note at the top of the list:* Press and hold the note, then press the Pin Note. Or slide your finger on the note and click on the pin.

❖ *Erase Note:* Slide left on the note and press the Delete Folder button. Or touch and hold a note and click on Delete.

If you have a change of heart, you can bring back the note by going to the "Recently deleted" folder.

You Can Look for Your Notes

You can look for typed and written text, things that appear in images, and writing in scanned documents.

1. In the list of notes, swipe the page to make the search field appear.

2. Tap the search field and type what you are looking for. You can also select a suggested search such as " notes with Sketching" and then enter another text to improve your search.

Only the title of a locked note appears in the search results if it is locked. The search integrates handwritten text (in supported languages), photographs, and scanned documents.

Search for Typed Text and Handwriting in A Note

1. Open the note that you want to search through.

2. Press the Actions button for notes, and then click Find in Note.

3. Enter the text you want in the search field.

CHAPTER 12

FACETIME

Set up FaceTime on Your iPad

Using FaceTime, you can make video and voice calls to family and friends, regardless of whether they have an iPhone or iPad or iPod touch, or a Mac computer. You can chat face-to-face with the front camera, or you can share what you observe by switching to the back camera. It takes a FaceTime Live Photo to shoot an exact second from your FaceTime discussion.

It's important to note that FaceTime, or at least part of its features, may not be available in all countries or locations.

1. To activate FaceTime, enter **Settings> FaceTime**.

2. Activate FaceTime Live Photos if you feel like taking pictures while on a FaceTime call.

3. To set up FaceTime, type your phone **number, Apple ID, or email address**.

You Can Call and Receive FaceTime Calls on iPad

You can call and receive through the FaceTime app by connecting to the Internet and using your Apple ID (first input your Apple ID or generate one if you don't have one).

You can use a cellular data connection to make a FaceTime call on iPad Wi-Fi + Cellular models, which may incur extra charges. To disable this feature, go to Settings> Cellular and disable FaceTime.

Call with FaceTime

Inquire of Siri. "FaceTime call Esther mobile," for instance.

1. At the top of the screen, click the Add button on FaceTime.

2. In the input area above, type your chosen name or phone number, then touch Video to make a video call or Audio to conduct a FaceTime voice call (not available in all countries or regions).

Tip: Turn your iPad to landscape mode to get a better view during FaceTime video chats.

From a Message Chat Begin a FaceTime Call

With the person you are discussing with you can begin a FaceTime call in a Messages chat.

1. Touch the profile pic, my account button, or the chat's top name in a Messaging conversation.

2. Press FaceTime.

Take A Facetime Call

When a FaceTime call comes in, choose one of the following options:

❖ *Accept:*
❖ *Decline:*
❖ *Remind me:*
❖ *Message:*

If a normal call comes in while you're on a FaceTime call, you'll get the End and Accept option instead of Accept, which denies the previous call and connects you to the new one.

Note: You can ask Siri to notify you when there is an incoming call, which you can receive or reject using your voice.

Shoot a Live Photo in FaceTime on the iPad

FaceTime Live Photo can be used to record a portion of a FaceTime video call (not available in all countries or regions). Anything that happens just during the shot is captured by the camera, including sound, so you can see and hear it afterward.

To capture a live FaceTime photo, go to Settings > FaceTime and turn on FaceTime Live Photos, then do the following:

❖ When you're on a call with someone else, use the Take Picture button.
❖ To view someone's face in a FaceTime Group chat, tap on their tile, then tap Full Screen, then Take Picture.

The Live Photo is saved in your Photos app, and you both receive a notification that it was shot.

Make a Group Call with FaceTime on Your iPad

You can call up to 32 persons to a Group FaceTime call using the FaceTime app (not existing in all countries or areas).

Launch a FaceTime Group Call

1. Click on the Add icon at the top of the screen in FaceTime.

2. Put the names or numbers of the people you wish to contact in the top field. You may also access Contacts and add contacts from there by tapping the Add Contact icon.

3. To begin a FaceTime video call, press Video, and to begin a FaceTime audio call, press Audio.

On the screen, each participant is represented by a tile. When someone talks (vocally or through sign language) or clicks the tile, it moves to the front and becomes more visible. Tiles that don't fit on the screen are visible at the end of a row. Slide down the row to find a person you don't see in the first place. (If an image isn't available, the participant's initials may display on the tile.)

Go to Settings > FaceTime, then turn off Speaking below Automatic Prominence to avoid the tile of the person speaking from getting larger during a Group FaceTime chat.

It's worth noting that detecting sign language requires the usage of a supported presenter model. Furthermore, all participants must be using iOS 14, iPadOS 14, macOS Big Sur 11, or a newer version of iOS.

Launch (start) a FaceTime Group Call from a Group Messages Discussion

You can launch a FaceTime Group call from a group Messages discussion with all of the members you're messaging with.

1. Toggle between the names or profile images at the top of the Messages chat.

2. Press the FaceTime button.

Adding a Second Caller

Any member can add another member at any instant during the meeting.

1. Touch the screen during a FaceTime conversation to display the controls (if they're not already showing), then swipe up from the top of the controls to press Add Person.

2. Type the name, Apple ID, or phone number of the person you choose to add in the top entry space. You can also use the Add button to add someone else from your Contacts list.

3. Touch Add Person to start FaceTime with somebody else.

Be part of a FaceTime Group Call

When you are asked to join a FaceTime Group call, you will be notified by the incoming call. If you decline the call, you will receive a notice stating that you can join the call at any moment while it is still in progress.

Quit a FaceTime Group Call

When a group chat is in progress, you can end it at any time by using the Leave call button.

If two or more people are still on the line, the call will continue.

During a FaceTime call on iPad, you Can Use Other Apps

While using the FaceTime app to make a call, you can make use of other applications.

Click on an app icon to open it on the Home Screen.

If you'd want to return to the FaceTime screen, simply click on the FaceTime icon in the top right corner.

Camera Effects is Now Supported in FaceTime Calls on iPad

FaceTime app can now be used to turn into your favorite Memoji or emoji character (on models with a TrueDepth camera) during a video call. A built-in filter has been added to change your appearance and add stickers, labels, and shapes on supported models. In FaceTime, you can take screenshots that include any special camera features you apply to a call.

Be a Memoji

Messages on an iPad with a TrueDepth camera allows you to create a Memoji character that you may use in FaceTime calls. Your movements, facial gestures, and voice are captured by the iPad and conveyed through your character. (Even when you thrust out your tongue, your character mimics you!)

1. Tap the Effects button while having a FaceTime call. (If the Effects button is not visible, touch the screen.)

2. Tap the Memoji button to choose a Memoji. They hear you, but they see your Memoji talking.

Use a Filter to Alter Your Appearance

1. During a FaceTime call on supported models, tap the Effects button. (If the Effects button is not visible, touch the screen.)

2. To access the filters, tap the Filters button.

3. At the bottom of the screen, you can alter your appearance by touching a filter (slide left or right to preview them).

Include a Text Label

1. In the middle of a call, click on the screen and then on the Effects button.

2. Tap on the Text button to pick a text label. Swipe up from the text window's top to reveal more label options.

3. Type the text you wish to appear in the label while the label is chosen, then click away from it.

4. Drag the label to the preferred destination. Pick the label you want to remove, and then click on the Done Editing button.

Stickers Can Be Included

1. During a call, press the screen, select the Effects button, and then select one of the following options:

❖ Press the Memoji Stickers button to add a Memoji sticker; press the Emoji Stickers button to add an Emoji sticker.

❖ Swipe up and touch the Emoji button after tapping the Text button.

2. To add a sticker to the call, tap it. To see additional options, swipe left.

3. Place the sticker where you want it. Tap the Done Editing option after selecting the sticker you wish to remove.

Shapes Can Be Added

1. During a call, press the screen and then click the Effects button.

2. To add a shape to the call, click the Shapes button, then tap a shape. Slide up from the top of the shapes window for more visible options.

3. Move the shape to the appropriate place by dragging it. After you've selected the shape you wish to delete, press the Done Editing option.

Block Unwelcome Callers in FaceTime On iPad

You can restrict unwanted callers' voice calls, FaceTime calls, and text messages via the FaceTime app.

1. Blocked Contacts can be found in Settings > FaceTime > Blocked Contacts.

2. Press Add New at the end of the list.

3. Choose a contact you'd want to block.

Swipe a contact or phone number to the left to unblock it, and then press Unblock.

Set the Camera to the Back Camera

If the controls aren't accessible, press the screen, then tap the Flip to Back Camera button while on a FaceTime conversation (tap it again to switch back to the front camera).

Disable the Audio

When on a FaceTime call, click the screen (if the controls aren't visible), then tap the Mute button (tap again to turn the sound back on).

Switch off FaceTime Call Camera

Press the screen, if the controls aren't visible, slide up from the top of the controls, and then tap Camera Off when on a FaceTime chat, click again if you want to turn it on.

CHAPTER 13

TIPS AND TRICKS FOR IPADOS 14

Apple stepped up its attempts to market the iPad as a productivity tablet with the release of iPadOS 13 last year. It considerably improved multitasking, offered desktop-class web surfing, and supported external drives, among other things. The Cupertino-based tech gigantic even went as far as to incorporate complete trackpad and mouse compatibility. This year, iPadOS 14 adds new features and augmentations to native iPad apps as well as the operating system as a whole. Let's move to the best tips and tricks you can use right now if you just update your iPad to iPadOS 14.

Stack Widgets in Today View

In Today View, iPadOS 14 bring restructured, resizable, and widgets with plenty of information. Besides, there's a Smart Stack of widgets that alternates based on usage configurations. Widgets can be managed by jiggling Today View.

However, rather than eliminating widgets, you can stack them in Today View to reduce clutter. Drag & drop widgets of comparable sizes on top of one another to do this. In terms of functionality, they'll be equivalent to the standard Smart Stack.

Apps Can Be Used From Any Location

With iPadOS 14, jiggling Home screen applications is a lot simpler. Rather than touching and holding any app icon, just long-press a space on the Home screen for a fraction of a second should work. This is likewise true for Today View.

Use Universal Search to Find Websites

The Search feature in iPadOS 14 has been given a makeover to make it look more like Spotlight Search on the Mac. It also works faster, makes better suggestions, and assists you in swiftly loading relevant results.

This restructured 'Universal' Search can work as an address bar; simply enter the URL of any website and click on Go to enter it in a new Safari tab.

Instead Of Typing, Write

Scribble, a fresh new feature in iPadOS 14, is a welcome addition. With Scribble your writing can be transformed to typed text in seconds, all you need to do is to start writing with an Apple Pencil anywhere that has a text field!

For example, instead of pecking away at the onscreen keyboard, you may now write your searches in Universal Search or Safari. Scribble gives you an almost limitless amount of options.

In the Notes app, choose the Scribble pencil (the one with the letter "A") from the tool menu and begin writing.

You Can Drag Out Apps for Multitasking

Do you wish to multitask with an app that isn't in the iPad's dock? Don't be concerned. If your iPad is connected to a keyboard, simply press Command+Space to launch Universal Search. Drag out the app you want to start in Split-View or Slide Over mode, in the results box.

This was also possible in iPadOS 13, but it's a fantastic (and little-known) feature worth highlighting again.

Perfectly Sketch Shaped Object

Sketching faultless shapes in the Notes app with an Apple Pencil is a snap. Simply start sketching and keep your Apple Pencil pressed down until the end and iPadOS 14 will identify and alter the form for you. This works with a variety of shapes, including lines, circles, rectangles, pentagons, and more.

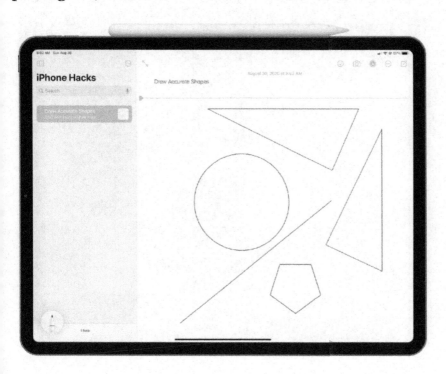

Apps That Invade Your Privacy Can Be Identified

iPadOS 14 brought a raft of new privacy and security features to the table, making it much more difficult for apps to snoop about your iPad. When an app accesses the camera or microphone, a green or orange dot appears in the status bar of the iPad.

Bring up Control Center to see which app is currently using (or has recently used) your camera or microphone.

Chose Handwritten Text

Handwriting detection in iPadOS 14 is so good that you may choose them just like typed text. By Double-tapping and using the selection handles you can highlight text.

Much better, you can copy and paste handwriting into other apps, and it will be instantly converted to written text.

Make Use of Scribble Gestures

With a variety of creative and exciting Apple Pencil gestures, iPadOS 14 makes Scribble super-convenient to use. The following are the best:

- ❖ **Scratch:** For deleting words you don't want.
- ❖ **Circle:** To pick words, phrases, or paragraphs.

❖ **Slice:** For generating or deleting spaces.

Use Safari to Translate Language

Surprisingly, the new Translate app from iOS 14 did not make it to iPadOS 14. It does, however, allow you to translate foreign websites in Safari by going to the **aA menu** and selecting **Translate to English**.

You Can Access Universal Search Without the Use of a Keyboard

The redesigned 'Universal' Search is so effective at finding apps, files, and photographs that it should be used everywhere. It's only available on the Home screen without a keyboard? Thankfully, AssistiveTouch is available as an alternative.

To access AssistiveTouch, go to Settings > Accessibility > Touch > AssistiveTouch. With a single-tap, double-tap, or long-press gesture you can activate Spotlight after enabling AssistiveTouch.

The floating AssistiveTouch circle can then be used to launch Universal Search whenever or anywhere you choose.

Items Can Be Dragged and Dropped into the Sidebar

The redesigned sidebars in native iPadOS 14 apps like Photos, Shortcuts, and Voice Memos are likely to have caught your attention. They don't only make it easy to go about. Rather, you can use them to swiftly move objects around — for example, you can drag & drop photos into albums from the Photos sidebar.

The Files app also allows you to move files using the sidebar, but you could do that on iPadOS 13 as well.

You can pin iMessage Conversations

Are you using iMessage on your iPad? It's now easier to join in on your favorite subjects. Swipe right on a conversation thread and tap the **pin-shaped icon**. With that, it can be pinned at the top of the urgency list. Up to nine pinned chats can be active at any given time.

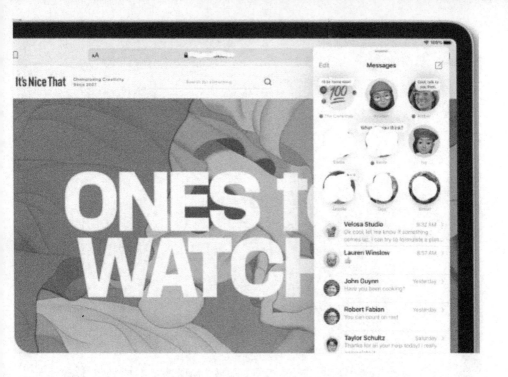

Use Apple Music's Autoplay Feature

The Music app in iPadOS 14 has been revamped with improved navigation and an immersive full-screen player. It also has a new Autoplay function that keeps the music playing even after an album or playlist is finished – open the Up Next list to activate or deactivate the feature.

You Can Take a Mirrored Selfies

Do you prefer to take selfies with your iPad? Head to
Settings > Camera and turn on the Mirror Front Camera
option to stop them from flipping the other way.

Rotate Photos Speedily in Files App

Photos can now be rotated without opening the Files app.
With the long-pressing of any image, you can choose to
Rotate Left or Rotate Right.

Deactivate Share Sheet Suggestions

Contact suggestions were added to the top of Share Sheets in iPadOS 13. If you don't like the added clutter, iPadOS 14 makes it simple to get rid of it. To do so, go to Settings > Siri & Search > Suggestions when Sharing and turn off the option next to it.

Boost the Quality of Your Voice Memos

The new Voice Memos software can boosts the quality of recorded voice memos and instantly eliminate background noise and echoes. Go to the Edit Recording screen and tap the wand-shaped Enhance Recording icon to do so fast.

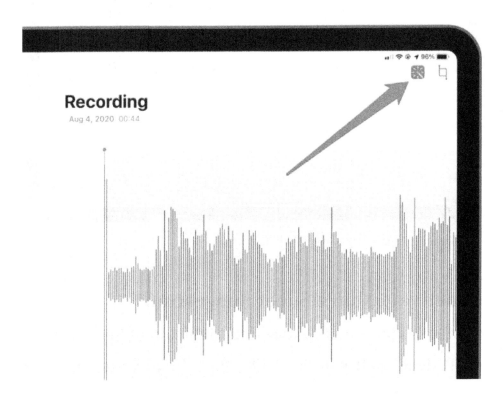

You Can Bring Up Emoji Picker

Simply tap the **Globe** key on a Smart Keyboard or a Magic Keyboard to bring up a handy emoji picture wherever the cursor is now located. This applies to any text area.

Siri Allows You to Send Audio Messages

When you call Siri on the iPad, she no longer takes over the entire screen. She's also a lot smarter, which complements her new compact style. For instance, Siri can record and send an audio message to a contact with you saying send an audio message to [Contact Name]. say Send, after Siri is done recording.

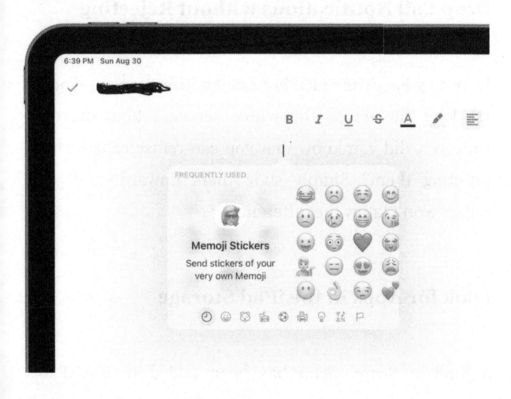

Blocked Access to the Photo Library

You don't have to give third-party apps complete access to your entire picture collection with iPadOS 14. You can instead limit exposure to specific photos or albums as needed. Go to Settings > Privacy > Photos to adjust your photo permissions.

Drop Call Notifications without Rejecting

Incoming FaceTime or iPhone call notifications in iPadOS 14 don't fill across the whole screen... long overdue! However, did you know that you can refuse calls without rejecting them? Simply slide them upward, and your callers won't know the difference!

Look for Apps in the iPad Storage

A built-in Search icon has been added to the iPad's storage management screen **(Settings > General > iPad Storage)**. To filter apps by name, tap it.

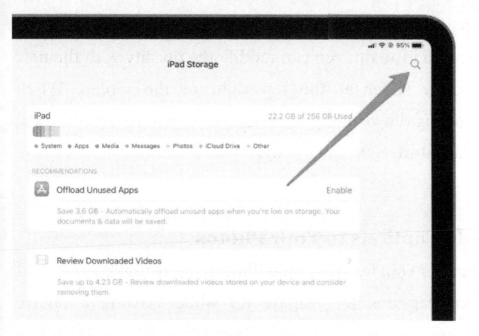

Change the Opacity of The Screenshot

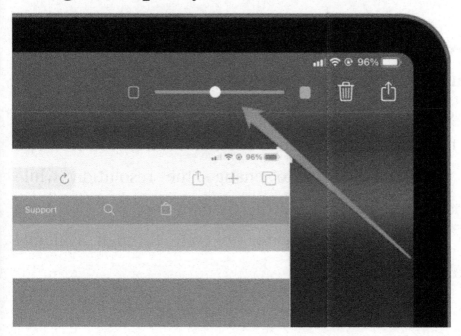

Do you use the iPad to annotate a lot of screenshots? Then here's a little tip: you can modify the opacity with the new Opacity slider at the top right of the screen. When boosting the visibility of annotations in noisy screenshots, this feature comes in handy.

Add Captions to Your Photos

Another cool feature of the Photos app is that you can add your captions by swiping up while viewing a photo. Syncing to other devices is possible if iCloud Photos is activated.

You Can Change the Video Quality in the Camera App

If you go to Settings > Camera > Record Video and turn on the option next to Video Format Control, you won't go to the Settings app to change the resolution while capturing videos. Within the Camera app, you can press the resolution/fps indicator to cycle through available quality settings.

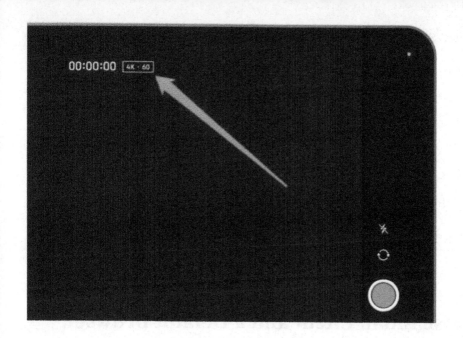

4K YouTube Is Available

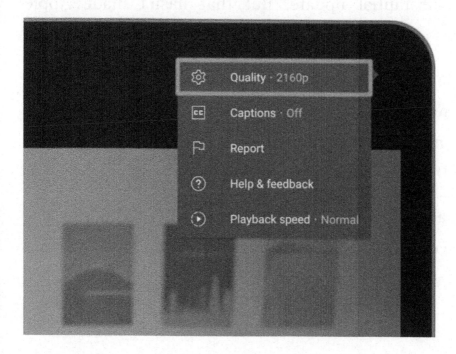

Google's VP9 codec is supported by iPadOS 14. That means you'll be able to watch YouTube videos in 4K on your iPad for the first time!

When you're watching a video in the YouTube app, go to the **Quality** menu and look for the 2160p option. This should work if you have iOS 14 downloaded on your iPhone.

Choose Email Client and a Default Browser

With improved privacy settings, a built-in translation module, and a faster JavaScript engine, iPadOS 14 Safari is a substantial update. But that hasn't made Apple restrict users from choosing their default browsers.

You may set Google Chrome as your iPad's default browser, for example, if you prefer it. Go to **Settings > Chrome > Default Browser App** and choose **Chrome** from the drop-down box.

This also applies to email clients, where you can use Gmail or Microsoft Outlook instead of the native Mail app if you want.

Enable History Stack

You can Long-press the **Back** option in a native app to bring up a stack of the previous pages anytime you're buried deep within many pages. Choose one so you can get to it fast.

Activate or Deactivate Precise Location

You can choose whether or not an app should have access to your precise location in iPadOS 14. Go to Settings > Privacy > Location Services to view the Location Services. Choose an app, then activate or deactivate **Precise Location** using the slider next to it.

Toggle to Dumb Stack

Do you find the Smart Stack widgets' auto-rotating feature annoying? You can stop it from doing that if you Long-press the stack, choose Edit Stack, and then toggle off the switch next to Smart Rotate.

Mask Your Mac's Address

Masking your iPad's MAC address in iPadOS 14 can make your privacy increase. Select a Wi-Fi network in the Settings app's Wi-Fi menu, and then switch on the option next to Private Address.

Siri Can Send an ETA Message

Siri also allows you to share your ETA with others. Saying Hey Siri in the Maps app and saying Share my ETA with [contact's name] can quickly share your E.T.A. with a contact.

Made in the USA
Monee, IL
14 February 2022

91275600R00095